PLEASE KNOCK!

written by
erin dolgan
M.A., LPC

illustrated by
john d. woods

EOZ Press

DENVER

For information, contact

EOZ Press

1221 South Clarkson Street, Suite 200

Denver, CO 80210

www.relativedanger.com

Please Knock

LCCN: 2006926682

ISBN: 0-9785628-2-8

Production Management by

Paros Press

1551 Larimer Street, Suite 1301   Denver, CO 80202

303-893-3332   www.parospress.com

Printed in China

1   3   5   7   9   10   8   6   4   2

Help me be safe.
Help me be strong.
Help me make good decisions,
And know right from wrong.

The world has become a scary place,
And way too much for a kid like me to face.
People we know, who we think are our friends
Sometimes may lead us to very bad ends.

So help me by sharing the thoughts in this book.
Let's turn the pages together and take a look!

please knock

Please...

Don't walk into my room without knocking first.

This is...MY area.

This is...MY space.

So...

I'll let you in,

But you should still ask.

I don't want to be surprised

When I see your face.

I am...

A KID

But I am still in charge of me.

So...

PLEASE KNOCK

And

ASK...

Before entering and

Scaring me.

dear mom and dad

I am sorry to say this,
Sorry to be such a drag,

But I need you to know,
I think I've been had.

I find it hard to say this because I am just a little kid,
And sometimes you miss the point
And say I'm imaginative.

But it's important to me, so LISTEN CAREFULLY!!
I tried to tell you, but the words wouldn't come out
Then my words flew and my voice was a shout.

You said, "not right now, later dear, our friend is coming for dinner."
So I wrote this letter.

Dear Mom and Dad,

You said to always be truthful about everything between me and you.
You said to yell and scream if I am in danger or something is bugging me.

So here it goes, your friend is not a friend of mine.
I don't like it when he visits our family from time to time.

I see him differently than you do.
I can't really say why or what for but,
I'd rather not have him around anymore.

Sincerely,

Your kid... best friends forever... let's talk later...
Maybe until midnight or half past four.

don't go changing

When I am changing out of my bathing suit,
I **WILL** choose where that will be!!
Even if my mom is in a rush,
I still don't want anyone to see.

I know we are late to gymnastics,
I know you drove as fast as you could.
But please don't make me put on my leotard in the car,
Just 'cause you think I should.

I know my mom always likes the skirts and dresses I have.
They are pretty but they don't always work for me.
I want to swing from the monkey bars,
Roll down the hill,
And climb a tree
Without leaving my underwear for everyone to see.

Please let me pick, where I change and what I wear.
It's MY CHOICE.
But, if you must choose, please be fair.
Let me be comfortable and safe;
That's all I care.

it's mine

Please don't tell me to wrestle with you,
This is MY body.

Please don't touch my hair,
It is attached to MY head.

Please don't try to hold my hand,
It is attached to MY arm.

Please don't squeeze my cheek,
It is attached to MY face.

Please don't tickle me,
MY body should approve first.

Please don't hug me,
I may not want to hug right now.

MY mind.
MY body.

I choose.

SO... I Know

SO... you are my coach,

But I know that you could be a little pushy or rude.

SO... you are my teacher,

But I know that you could still make mistakes.

SO... everyone says you are the nicest man,

But I know that you could ask me to keep a secret.

SO... you are part of my family,

But I know that you could tell me to do something that doesn't feel right.

SO... you are my tutor,

But I know you could still struggle to get the answer.

SO... you are my friend,

But I know that you may want things that I don't want.

SO... I KNOW

THAT ANYONE COULD MAKE ME FEEL UNCOMFORTABLE

And

I know
Who I CAN trust.

ME!

sam

Sam

Was plain and simple,

Liked long walks,

Had a white fence, big house

     and the greenest yard,

3 kids, 2 cats and a dog

     that didn't bark.

Sam had many friends

Who came over and stayed all day

And sometimes all night.

The neighborhood thought

     Sam was a good guy,

For hiring kids of all ages and types

To help work on his house.

The hours were long and hard,

But the pay was always large.

Lunch times were long and the food

     was the best by far!!!

Questions were never asked,

Because after all...

Sam

Was plain and simple,

Liked long walks,

Had a white fence, big house and the greenest yard,

3 kids, 2 cats and a dog that didn't bark.

Until one day it had gone too far.

Sam asked Bob, a loveable kid,

To pose for pictures and he did.

Sam wanted to take Bob's picture almost every day.

Dressing like a pirate,

May have been somewhat fun.

But Bob felt uncomfortable

When the posing for pictures was done.

Bob tried to get away.

He was tired of posing for pictures day after day.

But no one thought Sam could ever do any harm

Because

Sam

Was plain and simple,

Liked long walks,

Had a white fence, big house and the greenest yard,

3 kids, 2 cats and a dog that didn't bark.

growing up

When I grow up
I probably won't be
what YOU think
I SHOULD BE.
But you will still be proud of
ME.

TRUST ME
YOU WILL BE !

I might be an
Astronaut,
Doctor,
Artist
Or
Actor,
Or
Even a
Scientist who makes important discoveries.

If I were a **Rock star**
I'd
SCREAM AS LOUD AS I COULD AND WITH
ALL MY HEART AND ALL MY MIGHT!

JUST LET ME BE ME AND THEN YOU'LL SEE
WHO I AM
IS SIMPLY AND
BEAUTIFULLY ME!!!

mistakes

Adults are older than kids
This much is true.

But they can make mistakes
Just like I do.

Sometimes adults are right
And I am wrong.
Then I have to listen to their preaching
All night long.

There are also those times
When my words make more sense.
I know right from wrong.
I have common sense.

Adults can make bad choices
Just like you and me.

Adults are not perfect
Even if they want to be.

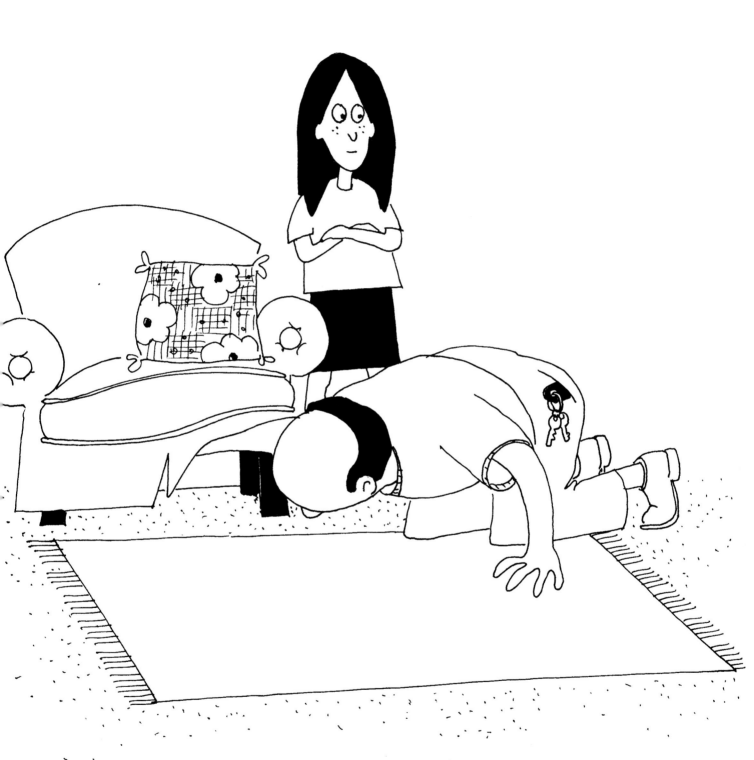

my body

I choose what to do with my body
And no one else.

Mommy told me to kiss her friend good-bye;
But I don't kiss if I don't want to.

Daddy says for me to give Grandpa a hug;
But I don't hug if I don't want to.

Mommy says at dinner that I have to sit next to someone she chooses;
But I won't sit there if I don't want to.

My mommy and daddy can choose to hug, kiss and whatever
But
I know what feels good
And
I know what feels weird

And sometimes, **I just don't want to.**

not even then

Just because

you're tall

doesn't mean you know it all.

Even if you're big

it doesn't mean you're the boss of me.

If I'm small

you still don't always know what's best for me.

Just because you think YOUR way is the way things should be

Doesn't mean I totally have to agree.

If you're a boy

doesn't mean

you should play with a certain kind of toy.

And

Girls don't always

have to look

all neat and pretty like a doll.

Even if you own three planets, the sun, the moon and the stars,

And are looking to buy the universe,

Just because you thought it might be fun.

NOT EVEN THEN!

Grownups.........Shouldn't always be trusted.

Even if they say

They must be.

BECAUSE

They've been around longer

And, they're older than a dinosaur.

NOT EVEN THEN, NOT EVEN THEN, NOT EVEN THEN!!!

shhh! it's not a secret.

When friends at school whisper it only makes me sad.

I wish they wouldn't tell secrets,

It only makes me mad.

Secrets are hurtful

And never for the best.

Kind of like coming in last place

Or failing a test.

So why do people whisper

Things that others can't hear?

Well,

our family gave up secrets.

In our house it's the golden rule.

Mom and Dad not excluded and...

Not to be cruel, but a rule is a rule.

We threw secrets out the window,

They'll never return.

Not even on a rainy day

Because...

They flew away.

Now, we use the word SURPRISE

Almost every day.

So when Mom or Dad say,

"shhh, it is a secret,"

correct them right away.

Remember!

Kick secrets out the back door

We don't need them any more.

Three or four surprises.

Anybody want some more?

respect

There are some things that are **private**

For most of us I think.

They are not really secrets

But they make my heart sink.

Yesterday my mom spoke to a lady in the grocery line.

She said that I broke a window.

My pitch is too strong

And now I'm paying the fine.

My father was in his office talking to a friend

Sharing how my little brother poops in his pants again and again.

My grandma told the clerk at the mall,

That I don't clean behind my ears.

So suddenly, I burst into tears.

Dad farted

during the family movie night,

But did I say anything?

     No.

I had no right.

Mom and Dad lose their keys at least 20 times a week.

But I never let this information leak!

I think what I'm saying is as clear as day;

Don't **talk about me** unless I say.

no friend of mine

My parents have a friend
Who comes over all the time
Who
Makes my dad laugh
And my mom smile as wide as a balloon.

But my parents don't know the creature the way I do.
He only makes me cry.
Telling me to not even try
To tell my mom and dad,
Even though I really want to.

To know that the truth is always best
Is the answer in this test.
They don't know what I know.
This sort of creature lies behind a hidden mask.

I'm scared.
I'm anxious.
I can't sleep
While the creepy creature creeps.

I'm TELLING my mom right away,
And my dad will understand and comfort me.
I am not waiting for 2 or 3 minutes of another day.

who can i go to?

Who can I go to...

When I have something to say?

It's not always the same person
From day to day.

Sometimes my mom is on the bed.
"I have a headache" is what she says.

I want to tell her something
That happened at school.
But, she is resting and I am losing my cool.

I could go tell my uncle,
He sometimes listens to me.

But he is yawning and ignoring
As far as I can see...

I think I'll call my auntie
Ring Ring on the phone.

She'll listen to what I have to say
But she's not home.

Oh, I see my uncle coming down the stairs
Just as I'm about to pull out my hair.

I ask him if he is rested and has time to spare.
He says, "for sure, you know I totally care."

Special appreciation and dedication to:

my husband, my best friend

Z.B., my best "gril"

Seth for giving rhythm to my words

my siblings for always being there

Jessica and Camilla for helping to make my dream come true.

You can purchase additional copies of *Please Knock!*
and find valuable information about protecting
and empowering your children at
www.relativedanger.com